Praying the Rosary with Sacred Art

MYSTERIES
MADE VISIBLE

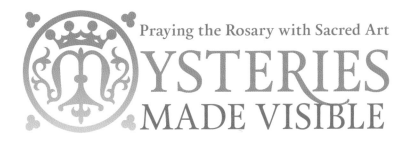

Praying the Rosary with Sacred Art

MYSTERIES MADE VISIBLE

Lawrence Lew, O.P.

IGNATIUS PRESS   SAN FRANCISCO

Nihil Obstat
Fr Neil Fergusson, O.P., S.T.L.
Censor deputatus

Imprimi potest
R. P. Martinus Ganeri, O.P., M.A., MPhil, DPhil
Prior Provincialis
Die 1 Septembris MMXXI

Cover art: The Rosary altar in the
Rosary Shrine church (St Dominic's Priory), London
Cover design by the Catholic Truth Society

Published by permission in 2022
by Ignatius Press, San Francisco
All rights reserved
ISBN 978-1-62164-584-9 (PB)
Library of Congress Control Number 2021950714
Printed in Italy ∞

Contents

FOREWORD

I believe in the power of prayer. I pray because I believe; I pray because I believe that without God I am powerless. We pray together because we believe in the power of community, of being in the Church, of being united as God's people.

If prayer is dialogue with God, how can the repetition of "Our Father" and "Hail Mary" be *dialogical*? Is the Rosary nothing but a mindless and monotonous monologue? But praying the holy Rosary is entering into a *dialogue with God.* The Lord's Prayer and the first part of the Hail Mary are part of the Gospel, the Word of God. Praying them allows us to listen, to ponder God's Word in our hearts. The first words of the Lord's Prayer invite us

to acknowledge the grace of being God's children, that we are brothers and sisters to one another. Each petition in the Lord's Prayer reveals a loving God who nourishes us, forgives us, delivers us from evil. The words of the Angel Gabriel "*the Lord is with you*" are words addressed to Mary and to us, for God is *Emmanuel.* It proclaims God's nearness to us. After listening to God's Word, we also address Mary: "Holy Mary, pray for us …". Then we glorify the Triune God: "Glory be to the Father and to the Son and to the Holy Spirit."

Mary of Nazareth became part of our lives because of three short but important "dialogues". The first is a dialogue with the Angel Gabriel: "Do not be afraid,

Mary.... Behold, you will conceive in your womb and bear a son, and you shall name him Jesus." And Mary said: "Let it be done to me according to your word" (*Lk* 1:26–37). This "dialogue" made Mary the *Theotokos*, the Mother of God. The second dialogue took place at the wedding at Cana: "My son, they have no more wine." Jesus seemed to hesitate: "my hour has not yet come"; but eventually granted the request of his mother who told the waiters: "Do whatever my Son tells you" (*Jn* 2:1–11). This "dialogue" clearly shows Mary as our intercessor who urges us to obey God, to be his disciples. The third dialogue is at the foot of the Cross: "Woman, behold, your son" (*Jn* 19:26–27). It seems less of a dialogue than a monologue for there was no audible response from a grieving mother; but, in the silence of her anguished heart, Mary must have repeated her response to the angel: "Let it be done to me according to your word." In this "dialogue" at the foot of the Cross, Jesus gave Mary to us, to be "our" Mother.

This book, *Mysteries Made Visible: Praying the Rosary with Sacred Art*, by our brother Fr Lawrence Lew O.P., Promoter General of the Rosary, invites us to a deeper understanding of the Rosary through his prayerful reflections and the sacred art that "preaches" each mystery of the Rosary. It invites us to enter into deeper dialogue with God. It invites us to participate, to join Mary in her dialogue with God.

Dialogue changes us, broadens our horizons of understanding. When old friends who turn into foes enter sincere dialogue, then they open the possibility for a restored and renewed friendship. When persons with different persuasions and beliefs enter into authentic dialogue, they open the path to understanding each other's point of view. When strangers welcome each other in dialogue, they begin to realise that the *other* is not so different after all.

Mary was "changed" in her loving dialogue with God, she became *Mother of God, intercessor* and *disciple, our Mother.* When we enter into a dialogue with God, we enter into prayer, a profound conversation with God that leads to a profound change, or in other words a conversion. When we enter into dialogue with others, a foe could turn into a friend, the *other* and stranger could become *familiar*: one who is not too different from ourselves; after all, we share the same humanity, we all belong to the family of God, *we are brothers and sisters*! This is an important truth that Pope Francis calls our attention to in his third encyclical letter *Fratelli tutti* (*On Fraternity and Social Friendship*). If humanity recognises that we have one Father and we are one family, humanity will not only survive but flourish.

Gerard Francisco Timoner III, O.P.
Master of the Order

INTRODUCTION

The Rosary is about life because the Rosary is about Jesus Christ and "in him was life, and the life was the light of men" (*Jn* 1:4). Indeed the Rosary is focussed on our deepest and most profound human flourishing, for the Rosary is about eternal life coming only from mankind's graced union with Christ as "from his fulness have we all received, grace upon grace" (*Jn* 1:16). In praying the Rosary, therefore, we choose life, and our hope is to share in the joys of Mary, the joys of eternal life with all the saints in heaven.

So, in the Rosary we contemplate the fulness of Christ's life, the mysteries of our salvation through his Incarnation, his Passion and dying and in his rising from the dead and returning to the Father. In the Dominican tradition the mysteries of salvation have been organised into three sets, and they form a great triptych in which we contemplate and see the astonishing divine plan of salvation: in the words of St Athanasius, "the Son of God became Man so that Man might become God" (CCC 460). In this triptych the work of salvation is thus unfolded: in the Joyful Mysteries we see God becoming Man, the joy of the Incarnation and of the fulfillment of ancient Israel's hopes. In the Sorrowful Mysteries we contemplate the depths of God's love for us, dying for sinners. St Thomas Aquinas reminds us that it is not the extent of Christ's sufferings that won our salvation but rather the intensity of his love, for one drop of Jesus's Precious Blood would have sufficed to redeem the world since God's love is infinite. So, in praying the Sorrowful Mysteries, we are brought to marvel at the depths of God's love made manifest in the Passion and Cross. And finally, in the Glorious Mysteries, we contemplate the effect of Christ's saving works, which is that mankind is now united to God in heaven, united in charity, and this glorious effect is seen first of all in the Assumption and Coronation of Our Blessed Mother, who is Mother of all the redeemed, Mother of the Church, the true Mother of all who live.

Since, as Pope St Leo the Great has said, "What was visible in our Saviour has passed over into his mysteries", i.e., the sacraments of the Church, so it is fitting too that the meditations of the Rosary should also include those aspects of the life of Christ called "the Mysteries of Light" by Pope St John Paul II. In 2002 that great Pope of the Rosary suggested that the five Luminous Mysteries might be added, as an option left open to the individual devotion and piety of the faithful, to the original fifteen mysteries that have been handed down in the Dominican tradition to the universal Church. These mysteries of St John Paul II, it seems to me, draw our attention to the sacraments "by which divine life is dispensed to us" (CCC 1131). This is an opportune moment for us to recall the unique and indispensable role of the sacraments in our Christian life. They are the ordinary means given to us by Christ through which we partake in the saving graces of his life, death and Resurrection. The sacraments are about our coming to life and being alive in Christ, united to his Mystical Body, the Church. So, in my reflections on the Luminous Mysteries, I have been drawn by grace to contemplate the sacramental significance of these mysteries, leading us, with those traditional mysteries of the Rosary, to contemplate the fulness of life that we have from God.

"The thief comes only to steal and kill and destroy; I came that they may have life, and have it abundantly" (*Jn* 10:10). There have been occasions in the history of salvation when our fulness of life in Christ has been particularly imperilled: historical situations and cultural circumstances which seem to be more allied to the thief than to the Good Shepherd. For error and heresy, as much as war, violence and corruption can effectively steal, kill and destroy our faith, thus potently severing us from our union with Christ, the sacramental life of the Church and the means of salvation and life. In particularly serious circumstances, the response of heaven has come through the Rosary. For the Rosary is about life, and it forms the mind in the truth of the Gospel, and so it conduces us to find eternal life through Christ and in the embrace of his holy Bride, the Church.

Therefore, at a time when the age-old heresy of dualism had imperilled the true faith, tradition holds that the Rosary, in a form that is recognisable to us as such, was introduced to the Church through St Dominic and his Order. Pope Leo XIII, with vigorous prose, recalls that in the 13th century "God's Holy Church suffered great trouble and grief from the Albigensian heretics, who had sprung from the sect of the later Manichaeans, and who filled the South of France and other portions of the Latin world with their pernicious errors, and carrying everywhere the terror of their arms, strove far and wide to rule by massacre and ruin." Hence both life and limb, body and soul were under threat in the Middle Ages due to the Albigensian heresy. For the Cathars, as they called themselves, were dualists, who posited the origin of the material creation as having come from an evil deity and who taught the need to free the spirit and soul from the body. Hence suicide was commendable (preferably by starvation), marriage and procreation were discouraged and the break-up of the family was exhorted. To counteract this movement against life and the family, several popes and saints recount that Our Lady gave the Rosary to St Dominic, telling him to preach her psalter, that is to say, 150 Hail Marys. Although the historical origin of the Rosary has been difficult for historians to verify, in the 15th century Blessed Alan de la Roche O.P. insists that the Rosary was given to St Dominic, and this would be repeated by St Louis Marie de Montfort and several popes. What we do know is that the Rosary as we know it, with its Joyful, Sorrowful and Glorious Mysteries, has long been regarded as the sacred inheritance and distinctive devotion of the Dominican Order, and it is this form of the Rosary that has been preached by the sons and daughters of St Dominic in words and devotions, in pious actions and in our sacred art and architecture.

Hence in 1571 the Dominican Pope St Pius V asked the Rosary Confraternity—a spiritual network of men and women who are affiliated to the Dominican Order and who have committed themselves to praying fifteen decades of the Rosary every week—to pray the Rosary, beseeching Our Lady to grant victory to the Christian armada assembled off the west coast of Greece at a place called Lepanto. At this time Christian Europe had been under threat as the Ottoman Empire had conquered swathes of formerly Christian lands. The vanquished people had to renounce Christianity and convert to Islam or be enslaved or killed. Countless people were deprived of the sacraments, and, had the battle at Lepanto been lost, all of Europe would have fallen prey to this darkness. But the light prevailed, and the Rosary was God's instrument of prayer that secured the fulness of life for Christian Europe. Pope St Pius V instituted a feast day in honour of Our Lady of Victory, and that day, 7 October, is now known as the Feast of Our Lady of the Rosary; 2021 marked the 450th anniversary of that victory, a victory made possible through devotion to the Rosary and the prayers of the Rosary Confraternity. The need remains in our own time for generous souls with pious faith to join the Rosary Confraternity and receive great favours from heaven for themselves, for their communities and for the Church. As Pope Leo XIII said, "From the Confraternities, the rest of the faithful will receive the example of greater esteem and reverence for the practice of the Rosary, and they will be thus encouraged to reap from it … the same abundant fruits for their souls' salvation."

More recently, in the 20th century, and on the brink of our own difficult times, in which the family and the Christian faith are much diminished and threatened, Our Lady of the Rosary appeared at Fatima and taught three shepherd children to pray the Rosary daily and to offer their spiritual sacrifices and penances for the conversion of souls. The message of Our Lady is simple: pray five decades of the Rosary daily. As Promoter General of the Rosary, I am conscious that the greatest promoter of the Rosary is Mary herself, and there can be no better endorsement, no greater encouragement, than to have the Queen of Heaven herself ask us to pray the Rosary every day.

But she does so with a mother's gentle love: without compulsion, nor guilt, nor under threat of sin. Rather she, the Mother of all who live, simply invites all of us who love life and who desire an abundance of life in Christ to heed her sweet words and so to offer her a crown of spiritual roses formed from our prayers and meditations on the mysteries of salvation contained in the Holy Rosary.

It is my hope that this book will be an encouragement and a help and an inspiration in your praying of the Rosary. The photographs were all taken by me in various churches around the world, and the photographs used in this book were selected by members of the Marian Devotional Movement based in Canada. Most of them are members of the Rosary Confraternity, and it has been a joy to pray with them online every Friday and to have them participate in the creation of this book in this way. Each of the photographs has been the basis for my meditations on the twenty mysteries of the Rosary. Together with Scripture, sacred art has inspired my thoughts and writing, giving rise to what has been called a *visio divina*, a theological rumination on a work of sacred art. Perhaps these will help you and inspire your own thoughts and stir up greater love for Christ and Our Lady. Certainly, my hope is that as you look at the photographs and pray the Rosary you will have your own theological reflections, the fruit of your contemplation of these Christian mysteries made visible.

TIPS ON PRAYING THE ROSARY

People often ask me how best to pray the Rosary, or they tell me that they've struggled with the Rosary and find it difficult. And some have thus given up on the Rosary. My own experience has also been one of struggle with the Rosary, and my mind wanders, I get distracted or I find myself just going through the paces but not really concentrating on the meditation. However, I find that having sacred art before my eyes does focus my mind. Nowhere is this more apparent to me than in my own Rosary Shrine church in London, where each mystery of the Dominican Rosary is depicted in sculpture or stained glass. As I walk from one Rosary Chapel to the next, slowly praying the Hail Marys, I enter these distinct chapels dedicated to each of the mysteries, and it is as though I am entering the mystery itself, and as I gaze on the sculpted tableaux, I find myself interacting with the art, the imagination is engaged, and the scenes come to life in my mind's eye. This engagement of intellect and imagination is vital, it seems to me, when we meditate on the Rosary, and my hope is that this book can guide us in doing so. Occasionally, music can also help to focus the mind.

The assumption of the Rosary Confraternity, too, which does not require its members to pray together physically, is that one can pray the Rosary alone, at one's own pace and in a place and manner of one's own choosing: pray it at home, sitting in the garden with your morning cup of coffee, kneeling by your bed, at school or in the office, while waiting for the train or bus, when standing in line or whenever you have spare moments. Very often we reach for our smartphones, but perhaps we can reach for our rosaries instead. As the Rosary was preached and used by itinerant Dominican friars, it seems likely that these beads are our mobile praying device to be carried on journeys and to be prayed as we travel from place to place. Many of my Dominican brothers have said that they prefer to pray the Rosary while walking. Praying the Rosary in this way, especially when we are using public transportation or walking down the street, is also a beautiful public witness of prayer, and it is a means of encircling our neighbourhoods and parishes with prayer.

However, I think it is most important that we do not overload ourselves by praying the Rosary all in one sitting. As St Thomas Aquinas said, we should stop praying when it becomes tedious and no longer increases our devotion. Pope Benedict XVI once said that he found it too intense to pray the Rosary all at once, and so he broke it up during the day, saying a decade or two now and again. St Louis de Montfort, although he encouraged groups to pray the Rosary together, also permitted busy people to pray just one decade at a time, for it is better to pray one decade well than to rush through five decades of the Rosary. My personal practice is to say a decade or two at a time, beginning the morning with a decade of the Rosary and offering the day to God. If you check your social media accounts, use this time as a chance to gather prayer intentions, and then pause and offer a decade or two of the Rosary for those intentions. In this way, before work, between meetings, in the middle of some writing or after cooking a meal, punctuate the day with more decades of the Rosary so that, as St Paul says, we can "pray at all times in the Spirit, with all prayer and supplication" (*Ep* 6:18). I usually aim to say at least five decades a day, but through this method of interspersing the day with the Rosary, I find that by the end of the day, I can often manage fifteen decades with relative ease. The day is thus suffused with thoughts of Christ and of his saving love for us; the heart thus increases in devotion for God; and so we are led by the Rosary to become more like our Blessed Mother Mary in our faith, in our hope and in our love. No wonder Our Lady has given us a daily prescription of five decades of the Rosary a day, because if each day is directed towards Christ in this way, then our whole life will be, like Mary's, surrendered to God's love. The Rosary, therefore, is for life because it leads us to the fulness of life, to union with him who is the Resurrection and the Life (*Jn* 11:25). Therefore, St Paul says: "Rejoice always, pray constantly, give thanks in all circumstances; for this is the will of God in Christ Jesus for you" (*1 Th* 5:16–18).

THE
JOYFUL
MYSTERIES

The Annunciation

And the angel said to her, "Do not be afraid, Mary, for you have found favour with God. And behold, you will conceive in your womb and bear a son, and you shall call his name Jesus."

✳ Luke 1:30–31 ✳

Heaven and earth are united in the Virgin's womb as the fiery light of the Holy Spirit descends from above. Divine light dispels the darkness of man's sins, shining fully on the one who is immaculate and irradiated with grace, filled with the fulness of God himself. Compared with her light, hailed as the one who is "full of grace", even the angel, who is rapt in wonder, kneels in the shadows. But the Virgin Mother is no goddess, she is not the Light but reflects the Sun like the Moon: "beautiful as the moon" as Scripture says of her (cf *Sg* 6:10). So the angel kneels in adoration of the God-made-Man in her womb; he kneels before the Temple of the Word. Mary, through her gestures, is shown treasuring and pondering in her Immaculate Heart the promises of God which she reads in Scripture (cf *Lk* 2:19). Through the Holy Rosary, she leads us to do likewise and to adore the loving God who has done "great things" for us (cf *Lk* 1:49, Our Lady's *Magnificat*), uniting the earthly sons of Adam to himself in heaven through the bridge that is the God-Man Jesus Christ. The Jesuit poet Gerard Manley Hopkins's fine translation of St Thomas Aquinas's eucharistic hym comes to mind as I gaze upon this scene: "Godhead here in hiding, whom I do adore,/ Masked by these bare shadows, shape and nothing more,/ See, Lord, at thy service low lies here a heart/ Lost, all lost in wonder at the God thou art."

THE VISITATION

Elizabeth was filled with the Holy Spirit and she exclaimed with a loud cry, "Blessed are you among women, and blessed is the fruit of your womb! And why is this granted me, that the mother of my Lord should come to me?"

✳ LUKE 1:41–43 ✳

In Mary's virginal womb, heaven and earth are contained, and those things which sin has kept apart are now united. For through his Incarnation the God-Man will achieve in himself the reconciliation of "all things, whether on earth or in heaven" (cf *Col* 1:20). God's work of salvation, therefore, is one of reconciliation and unity. God and his grace bring the disparate together, uniting in Christ that which sin and our fallen humanity have driven apart and divided. One of the divisions we find in our polarised world is between the generations, between youth and the elderly, and the two often do not see eye to eye. Mary and Elizabeth, both filled with the Holy Spirit, reveal the unifying power of God, and Mary, as Mother of the Church, shows us that the Church, being the Mystical Body of Christ, is moved by grace to reach out to heal any divisions caused by sin; to reconcile dichotomies introduced by misunderstanding; and to gather young and old to live and work together in peace, as we see in healthy parishes, religious communities and families. So, in Christ we shall be reconciled, if we are united to him by grace. Our common work of prayer, as we meditate together in the Holy Rosary on these mysteries of our salvation, shall draw us into a deeper spiritual communion with one another; together we look into the face of the Holy One of God who has first reached out to reconcile sinners to himself. Blessed indeed is the fruit of the womb of Mary, through whom we are so blessed. For "blessed are the peacemakers, for they shall be called children of God" (*Mt* 5:9).

The Nativity of the Lord

*For while gentle silence enveloped all things, and night in its swift course
was now half gone, your all-powerful Word leaped from heaven, from
the royal throne, into the midst of the land that was doomed.*

✳ Wisdom 18:14–15 ✳

Let our praying of the Rosary and our meditation of the mysteries of God's love be enveloped in silence and stillness. Even if the world bustles around us and the busy-ness of life urgently encroaches on our prayer, let the span of at least one decade of the Rosary be free of distraction and worry. Enter into the "cell of self-knowledge", as St Catherine of Siena calls it, that interior space in our soul where we will find also "the knowledge of God's goodness to you". And so in prayer and meditation we shall find ourselves, too, in that still small grotto of Bethlehem where God's superabundant goodness to mankind is made evident, made visible, made flesh and now dwells among us. For in the middle of the night, that is to say, as the deepest darkest shades surround us, so a great light has now shone. Even the stars descend to witness this marvel, but their light is unnecessary, rendered dim and faint by the brilliance of the One who is the world's true Light, the "Morning Star that never sets". A myriad of angels, too, crowd around even though they occupy no space, and so they gaze in awe of God's love that the limitless Creator of all should will to be bound by time and space and our humanity. In prayer, then, even if for a short time and in this place, let us bow our heads like the Virgin Mother's and so touch the unbounded love of God. For he has come to dwell with us. Indeed, the Dominican mystic Meister Eckhart thus reflects: "St Augustine says this birth is always happening. But if it does not happen in me, what does it profit me? What matters is that it shall happen in me."

THE PRESENTATION OF THE LORD

Inspired by the Spirit Simeon came into the temple; and when the parents brought in the child Jesus, to do for him according to the custom of the law, he took him up in his arms and blessed God.

✳ LUKE 2:27–28 ✳

The grain and patina of the wood permeates this scene, reminding us always of the noble matter of the Holy Cross: "Behold the wood of the Cross" rings out the cry on Good Friday in the Church's solemn Liturgy. And in the words of one of the most ancient hymns in praise of the Cross, "sweet is the wood, and sweet the nails sustaining the sweetest weight" of the Saviour. So in his prophecy (cf *Lk* 2:29–35), Simeon proclaims Christ to be the world's salvation, the One for whom all God's people have long awaited, but he also alludes to the costly price of our salvation, the sacrifice of Christ upon the wood of the Cross. St Joseph's gesture, cradling the sacrificial doves, who are symbols of innocence and purity, echoes the gesture of Simeon, cradling the innocent One who will become our true Passover Lamb. Anna, who represents the faithful women of Israel, of the Old Covenant, looks intently at Christ, her hands raised in the *orans* position, the ancient posture of prayer. For God's Chosen People, over many long centuries, have prayed for the coming of the Messiah, whom Anna now beholds with a gesture of wonder and deep joy. Mary stands for the New Covenant, for our Holy Mother the Church, and she too is rapt in prayer, her eyes fixed on the Redeemer, her hands pointing heavenwards towards God whom she calls "my Saviour" (*Lk* 2:47). With deep joy, too, the Church rejoices that God "has helped his servant Israel, in remembrance of his mercy" (*Lk* 2:54), and we continue to pray for the Jewish people that their eyes may see God's salvation, and so rejoice with Simeon and Anna.

The Finding of the Child Jesus in the Temple

The words of a man's mouth are deep waters; the fountain of wisdom is a gushing stream.

✳ Proverbs 18:4 ✳

The prophet Ezekiel prophesied that living water shall flow from the Temple to refresh and heal the world (cf *Ezk* 47), and this begins to be fulfilled when the Incarnate Word returns to the Temple, and he is found by Mary and Joseph to be there, seated among the teachers, and amazing them with his "understanding and his answers" (cf *Lk* 2:46–47). So, from Christ, the Wisdom of God, flows divine wisdom and knowledge and truth to refresh the world; issuing forth from the Temple, that is to say, from the place of worship and Sacred Liturgy, God's wisdom heals the world and brightens our minds darkened by sin and error. Thus the deep body of water behind the figure of Christ in this window and the light coming through the window similarly evoke the light of knowledge, the deep waters of wisdom and the divine illumination of the human mind that comes from listening to the Word of God, Jesus Christ. Our Lady, who silently "kept all these things in her heart" (*Lk* 2:51), is shown to be closest to Wisdom, intently looking at Christ, pondering his deeds: the Mother learning from her divine Son. Through the gift of her Rosary, Mary, the "seat of Wisdom", invites us her beloved children to contemplate with her the wisdom of her Son. She invites us to seek Christ, to love Truth and to learn from Jesus by pondering the Rosary's mysteries of God's saving love. For by searching for and meditating upon God's wisdom made manifest in Christ we shall, with joy, draw water from the wells of salvation (cf *Is* 12:3).

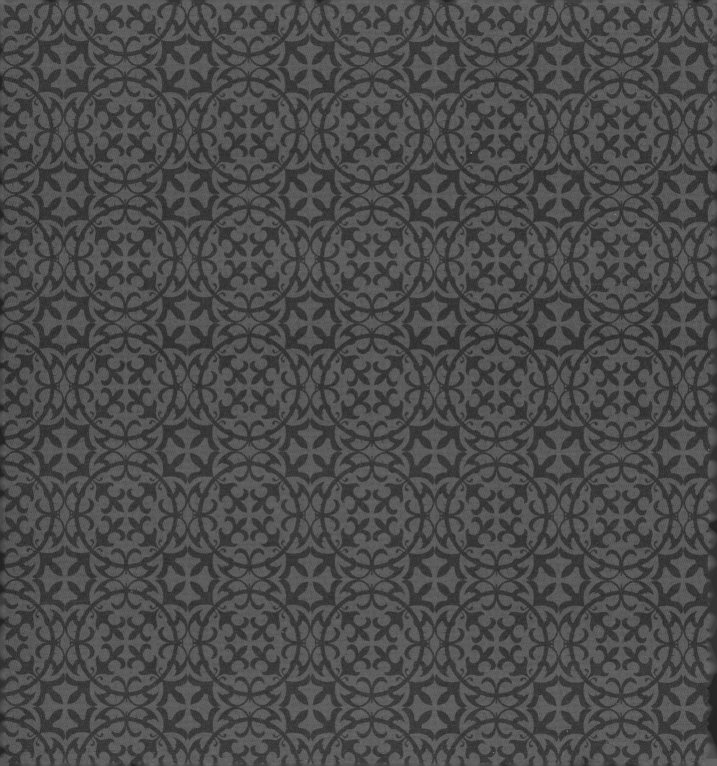

THE
SORROWFUL
MYSTERIES

The Agony in the Garden

Even though I walk through the valley of the shadow of death, I fear no evil; for you are with me; your rod and your staff, they comfort me.

✳ Psalm 22 [23]:4 ✳

A beautiful light suffuses this scene. For the living God, who has known and shared our pain in the person of Jesus, visits us daily with his divine grace to strengthen us and encourage us with hope in Christ's Resurrection, to bring his glory and light to our darkness. For this is the hour of Christ's glory (cf *Jn* 12:23). Hence, at Gethsemane, Christ repeatedly tells his disciples to pray. Our sufferings can wear us down and tire us out, or sin makes us drowsy and we struggle to stay awake, struggle to watch in hope for the salvation of God; so it is precisely in these times that we must pray. "Rise and pray", says the Lord (*Lk* 22:46). For many the familiar repetition of the Rosary and even just the fingering of the beads is about all the prayer we can manage sometimes. Thus the Rosary becomes for us God's "rod and staff" to steady us, to guide us forward through the "valley of the shadow of death", to bring us strength and comfort. In 1916, as the children of Fatima prayed the Rosary, the angel of peace, who would also come bearing a chalice, appeared three times to them. "Be not afraid", the angel told them, and then he taught them to "accept and bear with submission the suffering" which God permits us to receive in life, offering our sufferings with Christ's agonies for the conversion of sinners. So in our Gethsemane moments may we be united in prayer to the Redeemer, dying with him that we might rise with him (cf *Rm* 6:8). For thus we share in the glory of the Living Lord who transcends suffering and death.

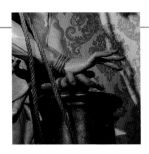

The Scourging at the Pillar

He was wounded for our transgressions, he was bruised for
our iniquities; upon him was the chastisement that made us
whole, and with his stripes we are healed.

✳ Isaiah 53:5 ✳

"Behold the man", declares Pilate (*Jn* 19:5) as he presents the crowds with this appalling sight. Behold, the gentle Lamb of God so harshly prepared for sacrifice! Behold, the merciful Redeemer so ruthlessly dealt with by his creatures! Behold him who thus takes away the sins of the world! Looking upon sweet Jesus wounded by man's violence is difficult, and yet we thus contemplate and ponder the depths of Christ's love for us sinners. The prophet Isaiah observes that Christ is the "man of sorrows . . . from whom men hide their faces" (*Is* 53:3). Many, indeed, would rather hide their faces from the suffering Christ and from the ongoing sorrows of humanity. Just as Adam and Eve once hid their faces from God, ashamed because of their rebellion against God's goodness, so now sinful men and women existentially hide from God and from the misery of our fellow men and women, not wanting to confront the costliness of sin. However St Paul says, "for our sake [God] made him to be sin who knew no sin" (*1 Cor* 5:21), and this is what sin looks like: sin lacerates us, wounds us deeply and leaves us bleeding and dying. Hence God becomes incarnate so that in his body he might lovingly bear the burden of our sins. St Catherine of Siena says: "I will hide myself in the wounds of Christ crucified, and bathe myself in his Blood and so shall my iniquities be consumed, and with desire will I rejoice in my Creator." So with sorrow we behold him who takes away the sins of the world, but we rejoice in our salvation for "by his wounds we have been healed" (cf *1 Pt* 2:24).

THE CROWNING WITH THORNS

And the soldiers plaited a crown of thorns, and put it on his head, and arrayed him in a purple robe; they came up to him, saying, "Hail, King of the Jews!" and struck him with their hands.

✴ JOHN 19:2–3 ✴

"We have no king but Caesar", shout the crowds (*Jn* 19:15). Time and again, through the moral choices we make, through the influencers and politicians and pundits we listen to, through our attraction to the powerful and wealthy of this world and our willingness to imitate their ways, we often cry out like those crowds did, and we give our obeisance to a king other than the one seated here in dignified solitude. But his is not a kingdom of this world. Rather, Christ's kingship is declared when we seek and strive after truth and life, holiness and grace, justice, love and peace (cf the Preface for the Feast of Christ the King). Christ's kingship transforms how we are to regard this world so that it reflects the heavenly reality of a person's true worth and dignity. Hence, the nobles in the court of the true king will consist of those who are "hungry or thirsty or a stranger or naked or sick or in prison" (*Mt* 25:44). These are, as the Order of Malta calls them, "our Lords, the Sick and the Poor". We, the servants of Christ the King, therefore, are to be found serving them through works of love that restore justice, uphold life and proclaim the sacral dignity of the human person. To mock the refugee, to ignore the poor and to neglect the needy, therefore, are tantamount to striking the King in the face. For in the faces of the least in our society Christ teaches us, through prayer and through his grace, to see his own "sacred head, sore wounded, defiled and put to scorn." In the least of our brethren we might indeed behold the Man.

The Carrying of the Cross

And yet ours were the sufferings he bore, ours the sorrows
he carried. But we, we thought of him as someone punished,
struck by God, and brought low.

✳ Isaiah 53:4 ✳

The Roman soldier holds the *fasces*, a symbol of imperial power and justice; a brutal bundle of rods bound by leather to an axe head that symbolises worldly authority. They remind us that our human laws and the execution of justice are often effected by fear, force and punishment. Hence the soldier points towards the Innocent One whom many consider to be a criminal. He too carries a brutal instrument of execution which has been laid upon him as he soldiers up the hill towards Calvary. But because of who it is who carries the Cross—God incarnate—so this wooden instrument of torture is being transformed from a sign of the punitive power of the State into a sign of the profound depths of God's humility, mercy and love for sinful humanity. So the Cross manifests the power of almighty God whose greatness is revealed in his lowliness, willing to accept even the humiliating death of crucifixion for our sake. The Cross also manifests the justice of God who takes upon himself the just penalty of suffering and sorrow incurred by our sins. Thus the Cross demonstrates above all "the breadth and length and height and depth" of God's merciful love "which surpasses knowledge" (*Ep* 3:18–19). As St Thomas Aquinas says, "God's wisdom was most evident in his preserving the order of justice and of nature, and at the same time mercifully providing man a saving remedy in the incarnation and death of his Son." So as we ponder Christ carrying the weight of our sorrows, our sins, our sufferings, we are uplifted by "Christ the power of God and the wisdom of God" (1 *Cor* 1:24).

THE CRUCIFIXION AND DEATH OF OUR LORD

I will pour out on the house of David and the inhabitants of Jerusalem
a spirit of compassion and supplication, so that, when they look on him
whom they have pierced, they shall mourn for him, as one mourns for an
only child, and weep bitterly over him, as one weeps over a first-born.

✹ ZECHARIAH 12:10 ✹

The compassion of God is so complete that the Crucified Christ is identified not just with the poor and the sick, nor only with victims and the suffering, but even with sinners. As St Paul says, "For our sake God made him to be sin who knew no sin" (*2 Cor* 5:21). Christ identifies with the sinner because the sinner is spiritually poor and sick; he is a victim of the errors and ignorance of this world, and his suffering is profound because sin deprives him of heavenly joys and of the blessedness of being united to God in love. Therefore Christ is crucified outside the walls of the city as an outcast; he hangs between two violent thieves, placed alongside criminals; and as "the wages of sin is death" (*Rm* 6:23) so Christ our God wills to die as we all must. How perfectly, therefore, does God identify with sinners: Behold the man! Behold

the compassion of God. Behold him who takes away the sins of the world! Contemplating the Crucified Lord every night, St Dominic wept for love of Christ. But he also cried out, "My God, my mercy, what will become of sinners?" St Dominic thus received "a spirit of compassion and supplication", weeping for sinners as for his own children, mourning because the obstinate sinner is the most pitiable of all people. Such sorrow for sinners and their plight energised the preaching of St Dominic, who strived to enlighten the darkness of error with reasoned arguments and with the truth of the Gospel. By meditating as he did on the mysteries of the Lord's Passion and Cross, our Dominican mission shall remain a work of mercy born of Christ's compassion and love.

THE
GLORIOUS
MYSTERIES

THE RESURRECTION

But the angel said to the women, "Do not be afraid; for I know that you seek Jesus who was crucified. He is not here; for he has risen, as he said. Come, see the place where he lay."

✳ MATTHEW 28:5–6 ✳

Death cannot contain Life. As the Easter Sequence says, "Mors et vita duello", "Death and Life struggled in a wondrous war, the dead Lord of Life reigns and lives". Hence the closure of the tomb is cracked open, and the grave itself stands empty, but it resembles an open door. As the Preface of the Dead intones, "for your faithful, Lord, life is changed not ended", so thanks to the Risen Lord Jesus and in union with him, death becomes the gateway to eternal life. Truly, henceforth, we need not be afraid, even in the face of death—not if we have faith in the Resurrection and are united to Christ through love. The women who came to the empty tomb early on the first Easter morning were seeking Christ with hearts full of love. We who pray the Rosary can do likewise, seeking the Lord with loving, attentive hearts. The invitation to come and see the place where he lay is an invitation to faith, to believe, to trust in God's Word. The women's hands gesturing towards this place are likewise inviting us to believe in the power of God to conquer sin, death and all that would terrorise us. Fittingly, this mosaic image does not show Christ climbing out of the tomb, as so many later images of the Resurrection would do. Rather, it has the reticence of the Gospel. The Resurrection is not seen by human eyes but is based on the testimony of others. Thus are we invited to faith, to trust in the word of others, and above all in the Word of him who is called the "faithful and true Witness" (*Rv* 3:14).

SECOND GLORIOUS MYSTERY

THE ASCENSION

As they were looking on, he was lifted up, and a cloud took him out of their sight.

✹ ACTS 1:9 ✹

Some say that seeing is believing, but we Christians "walk by faith, not by sight" (*2 Cor* 5:7). So before his ascension Jesus gives these final words to his disciples: "I am with you always, to the close of the age" (*Mt* 28:20). St Matthew's Gospel account ends here, but the good news of salvation continues in the history of the Church, in the stories of each of Christ's followers down to each one of us who also must walk by faith, believing not because we have seen the Lord with our eyes, but because we trust his Word, because of who he is. Hopkins's translation of St Thomas Aquinas's eucharistic hymn *Adoro Te devote* says, "Truth himself speaks truly or there's nothing true." So the Lord's ascension into heaven does not mean that he is absent. Rather, he is taken from our sight so that we can learn to believe without relying solely on our bodily senses. For faith is "the assurance of things hoped for, the conviction of things not seen" (*Heb* 11:1); faith is believing and relying on the Word of God's Son. Thus Mary and the apostles return to the Upper Room in Jerusalem where Christ had instituted the Eucharist. There, they recalled the words of the Lord, and they remembered his promise to be with the Church always, and so they gazed not up into the sky any longer but, with faith, they gazed upon heaven contained in the Host. For Christ has ascended into heaven to prepare a place for us (cf *Jn* 14:3), and in the Eucharist we have a foretaste of its chief joy, namely, union with God. After his ascension Christ is now present to us even more intimately than before.

The Descent of the Holy Spirit

Suddenly a sound came from heaven like the rush of a mighty wind,
and it filled all the house where they were sitting. And there appeared
to them tongues as of fire, distributed and resting on each one of them.
And they were all filled with the Holy Spirit and began to speak in
other tongues, as the Spirit gave them utterance.

✳ Acts 2:2–4 ✳

Christ is the Word, but the Spirit is the One who gives us speech. It is the Spirit who causes us to cry out "Abba, Father" (*Rm* 8:15); the Spirit who will teach us what to say (*Lk* 12:12); the Spirit who will give us eloquence and wisdom in speech (cf *Lk* 21:15). Thus, when the Spirit comes from heaven, he is seen like tongues "as of fire". Although it's often said that the Holy Spirit descended like flames from heaven in order to inflame us with divine love, it seems more likely that the Holy Spirit descended in tongue-like form, and these moved and flickered like a flame. St James likewise likens the tongue to a fire (cf *Jm* 3:6) because what we say can be destructive of relationships and inflame the passions, inciting anger, hatred and violence. God's Spirit, however, is "a spirit of power and love and self-control" (*2 Tm* 1:7). Therefore, when the Spirit comes to us, he will bless our speech and move our tongues, not like a passion-driven wildfire but with self-control, with reason, shedding light on situations and arguments like the peaceful illumination of candlelight. The Holy Spirit will inspire us to utter words that will powerfully move the hearer to love, and love is a rational, willed act. For the Holy Spirit gives us speech, he gives us to speak the Word of God; and God's Word is Love. Thus "the fruit of the Spirit is love, joy, peace, patience, kindness, goodness, faithfulness, gentleness, self-control" (*Ga* 5:22–23).

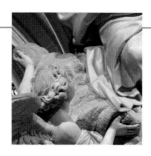

The Assumption of Our Lady

For lo, the winter is past, the rain is over and gone.
The flowers appear on the earth, the time of singing has come....
Arise, my love, my fair one, and come away.

✳ SONG OF SONGS 11–12A, 13B ✳

The Archangel Gabriel was transfixed by the Immaculate Virgin when he first hailed her. In the words of a Byzantine text sung at Matins on Sundays, "Awed by the beauty of your virginity and by the splendour of your purity, Gabriel cried aloud to you, Mother of God: How can I praise you as I should? By what name shall I invoke you? I am troubled and amazed. Therefore, as I was commanded, I cry to you: Hail, full of grace!" This plenitude of grace in Mary is precisely that which preserved her from sin, and, at the close of her earthly life, preserves her from the corruption of the grave. So her eyes look ever upward towards the Most High God whose grace had overshadowed her; her arms thus opened to embrace his will with her eternal *fiat*. Hence the angels are transfixed and gaze in wonder upon her, God's most beautiful creature, as she is raised from the grasp of death. The apostles too gaze in joy, seeing their Mother share in her Son and Saviour's glory. And the Church looks on with hope at the marvellous sight: behold, our Mother and model raised to heavenly heights, summoned by God to "come away" to true life after the rainfall of this "vale of tears" and the freezing winter of death. Therefore, all of creation rejoices to see the fruit of redemption: where Eve's fruit brought death, the New Eve brings eternal life. So, in the Divine Liturgy of St Basil the Church sings the words of St John Damascene: "In you, O woman full of grace, the angelic choirs, and the human race, all creation, rejoices!"

THE CORONATION OF OUR LADY AS QUEEN OF HEAVEN AND THE GLORY OF ALL THE SAINTS

At your right hand stands the queen in gold of Ophir. Hear, O daughter, consider, and incline your ear ... and the king will desire your beauty.

✳ CF PSALM 45:9–11 ✳

The whole of heaven is assembled for a wedding celebration, and the Mother becomes the "Bride Unbrided". For, full of grace, Mary is both Mother of God and also the Spouse of God. As such she represents all the saints, all the Redeemed of Christ, all those who, by grace, have been united to God in perfect charity; in a love more intimate even than a marital bond. The nuptial love of husband and wife is but a sacramental sign pointing to the eternal bond of love between Christ and his holy Church. The immaculate Virgin Mary, therefore, stands for the Bride of Christ "without spot or wrinkle, holy and without blemish" (cf *Ep* 5:27); the Church Triumphant in heaven. Kneeling before her Son and Redeemer, Mary receives from Christ a crown, symbol of all the merits and graces she has received from God. For as St Augustine said, in crowning our merits God is crowning his own gifts since, in the order of grace and salvation, all we have comes from God—all is gift because apart from Christ we can do nothing (cf *Jn* 15:5). Since Mary is greatest in charity, with her halo as red as Christ's, so she is closest to God, and rightly crowned as Queen of Heaven, Queen of All Saints, Queen of all those who, by grace, are united to God in eternal love. Meditating in the Holy Rosary upon her glory, which is Mary's ardent love for God, we pray that she will help us grow in charity, and so become closer to God. Through works of love now, may we don the wedding garment of good works and mercy, and so be prepared for the wedding feast of heaven (cf *Mt* 22:12).

THE
LUMINOUS
MYSTERIES

The Baptism of the Lord

And when Jesus was baptised, he went up immediately from the water, and behold, the heavens were opened and he saw the Spirit of God descending like a dove, and alighting on him; and lo, a voice from heaven, saying, "This is my beloved Son, with whom I am well pleased."

✴ Matthew 3:16–17 ✴

The shell is a symbol of pilgrimage. It stands out in this sculpted depiction of Christ's baptism because it is the only aspect that differs from the biblical account, and as such it recalls our own baptism by which we participate in Christ's baptism; for Christ went down into the waters of the Jordan, a foreshadowing of his descent into the dead in order to rescue humanity from death. So, through baptism we are led from the death of sin to new life in Christ, from darkness into light (cf *1 Pt* 2:9). For many centuries it was the common practice for Christians to be baptised by immersion in living water, a sign of dying and rising with Christ (cf *Rm* 6:4). Nevertheless baptism by affusion, i.e., by the pouring of water three times over the head, is mentioned in the 1st century *Didache.* It becomes symbolic of the outpouring of the Holy Spirit, whose radiance and light fills this scene. Baptism was thus also known in the early Church as "enlightenment" because the Christian is regenerated by the light of habitual grace which fills the soul; we are reborn in the image and likeness of the beloved Son, the Light of the World, who thus says to us: "You are the light of the world" (*Mt* 5:14). Baptism, therefore, inaugurates our Christian pilgrimage; it sets us on the way as pilgrims with a mission and a destination. With the Word of God as the light for our path (cf *Ps* 119:105) we are told that on our journey to our true home we must "let your light so shine before men, that they may see your good works and give glory to your Father who is in heaven" (*Mt* 5:16).

The Wedding at Cana

On the third day there was a marriage at Cana in Galilee, and the mother of Jesus was there.... His mother said to the servants, "Do whatever he tells you."

✳ JOHN 2:1, 5 ✳

A 5th century hymn for the feast of the Epiphany marvels that at Cana, "By a miracle divine, the water reddens into wine: Christ spoke the word, and forth it flowed in streams that nature ne'er bestowed." The miracle of Cana, alluded to by the crimson tones in this image, is the first of Jesus's signs, and it discloses the great work of Christ's grace which is to elevate and transform our human nature so that it may be joined in friendship to the Divine Nature. Christ sanctifies us, he divinises us, and so the water of our humanity is reddened by the wine of his divinity. Our union with God through grace, through charity, is the love shared between friends (cf *Jn* 15:15). And marriage, St Thomas Aquinas reminds us, is the greatest of friendships on earth, and so it becomes a potent sign of Christ's love for

his Church, for us. No one knows this better than Our Lady, for her union with God is so intimate and deep because she has united her will to God's. "*Fiat*" (*Lk* 1:38), she responded to the archangel, and here she spells out its meaning and gives us her motherly instruction: "Do whatever he tells you." This surrender to God's providence and mysterious will is not easy, just as marriage, and striving for unity of heart and mind and daily fidelity is challenging and arduous. The way of love takes us up the way of the Cross to Calvary. Hence Jesus must be invited into our marriages and into our lives to transform the water of our actions into wine, new works of charity. Just as at Cana, so too in our current circumstances, he comes by grace. "And the mother of Jesus was there" too (*Jn* 2:1).

The Proclamation of the Kingdom of God

Jesus came into Galilee, preaching the gospel of God, and saying,
"The time is fulfilled, and the kingdom of God is at hand; repent,
and believe in the gospel."

✳ MARK 1:14–15 ✳

God has drawn near to our humanity, and nothing is too obscure or unworthy for his mercy and love. So Christ came into Galilee, indicated by the sea in the background of this image. Galilee was considered to be a rural backwater, a region regarded as being polluted by the pagan practices of Gentiles (cf *Mt* 4:15). Even the Apostle Philip had wondered, "Can anything good come out of Nazareth?" (*Jn* 1:46). Yet it is precisely here that Jesus grows up and begins preaching the Kingdom of God, bringing the light of truth and of grace into the darkness. For this is what it means to be called to repent: it is a call to broaden our horizons, to open our eyes and minds and hearts so that we can see things as God does and to love what he loves. This is what friendship with God gives us. And so, in order to call us to such heights,

Christ first comes down into the Galilee of our lives, into the ordinary and hidden places of our hearts, even into those situations of sin and sickness where no good can seem to come from them. The people are depicted flocking to him, their eyes transfixed, so we too must look to him in trust and go to him. The sacraments of healing are where we encounter Jesus who has come to befriend us and to lead us from the shores of Galilee to the shores of heaven. So, inside the confessional the prophecy of Isaiah is fulfilled: "The people who sat in darkness have seen a great light" (*Mt* 4:16). Through Confession and Anointing the Gospel of God's mercy, the good news of salvation is being proclaimed. Indeed, God's Kingdom is thus actualised in our lives.

The Transfiguration

We were eyewitnesses of his majesty. For when he received honour and glory from God the Father and the voice was borne to him by the Majestic Glory, "This is my beloved Son, with whom I am well pleased", we heard this voice borne from heaven, for we were with him on the holy mountain.

✺ 2 Peter 1:16–18 ✺

If it is at our baptism that the Father declares each of us also to be his beloved son and daughter—beloved through the giving of the Holy Spirit of Love who dwells in us—so it is in our confirmation that the Father's voice is heard once again: calling us through grace to live as his beloved children, strengthening us still more with a fresh revelation of his Spirit of divine Sonship (cf *Ga* 4:6). Hence on the holy mountain "a bright cloud overshadowed them" (*Mt* 17:5), conveyed in this mosaic through the golden light that suffuses the entire scene. As the Holy Spirit also overshadowed Our Lady and made her the unique bearer of the living Word of God, so every Christian, baptised and confirmed and thus filled with the Holy Spirit, is also called to become a bearer of God's Word to the world. "For so the Lord has commanded us, saying, 'I have set you to be a light for the nations, that you may bring salvation to the uttermost parts of the earth'" (*Ac* 13:47). But we cannot bring that which we have not seen and experienced. So every week we need to climb the holy mountain for, through the sacraments, we hear Moses and Elijah: the Law and the Prophets and the Gospels being proclaimed in the Mass. In the Holy Eucharist we see the majesty of God and receive once more the gift of divine love that draws us closer to God so that we become spiritually eyewitnesses of the living God. For he has called us up the holy mountain with him so that we can descend into the valleys and roads during the week and to our peers become a bearer of good news and light.

The Institution of the Holy Eucharist

For their sake I consecrate myself, that they also may be consecrated in truth. I do not pray for these only, but also for those who believe in me through their word, that they may all be one; even as thou, Father, art in me, and I in thee, that they also may be in us.

✳ JOHN 17:19–21 ✳

"Thy cradle here shall glitter bright, and darkness glow with newborn light" goes St Ambrose's Christmastide hymn. And then, towards the end of Christ's life, another hymn by Venantius declares: "The Cross shines forth with mystic glow." The light of the Lord's Incarnation and Cross is concentrated now in the Holy Eucharist: it shines out with golden rays. Christ gives us himself in this wondrous Sacrament so that his light might ever brighten our days, guiding our pilgrim footsteps forwards; and enlighten our minds with his promise: "Lo, I am with you always, to the close of the age" (*Mt* 28:20). The mysteries of creation, Incarnation, the Church, her sacraments, and of grace all declare that God is with us. God has promised never to abandon us, never to let the darkness engulf us, never to forget us. All this is contained in the Host, for in the Eucharist, God has given us his Word. Hence the Eucharist is the Mystery of Faith: it summons us to dare to believe in the promises of Christ. And faith, for those who have the courage to believe, is a light that draws us forward through life; true light coming from the One who has risen and conquered sin, suffering and death. The Eucharist is our light from him who is *"lumen de lumine"*. The Holy Rosary, prayed in faith in union with Mary, the Woman of Faith, is our lamp for the Christian's heaven-bound journey: it fills the mind with salvation's light and fills the soul with God's grace and love. The Rosary is for life, leading us to Life. Thus may Our Lady of the Rosary make us worthy of the promises of Christ!

How to Pray the Rosary

In the Dominican tradition, the Rosary essentially consists of three simple prayers: the Lord's Prayer, the Hail Mary, which is said ten times to form a "decade", and the Glory Be. The mysteries of salvation are grouped into sets of five, as shown in this book, and these are called the Joyful, Sorrowful and Glorious Mysteries. In 2002, Pope St John Paul II suggested that the Luminous Mysteries could be added to these. Nevertheless, the traditional Dominican Rosary consists of fifteen mysteries, which is why the Rosary Confraternity is currently still bound only to the recitation of fifteen mysteries a week.

The manner of beginning the Rosary allows several variations, which Pope St John Paul II explains in chapter III of his encyclical *Rosarium Virginis Mariæ*. The Dominican tradition, which is followed by the Legion of Mary, is to treat the Rosary like the Divine Office and so one begins with "O Lord open our lips ... O God come to our aid." A universal custom, which is reflected in the Rosary beads themselves, is to recite the Apostles' Creed and then say one Our Father, three Hail Marys and one Glory Be for the intentions of the Pope.

The heart of the Rosary, though, comes not merely from saying the prayers, but from meditating on the mysteries. This book, therefore, hopes to provide an aid to meditation, and the aim of this

Second Mystery
Our Father
Begins 2nd Decade

Glory Be

Ten Hail Marys

End

First Mystery
Our Father
Begins 1st Decade

Glory Be

Three Hail Marys

Our Father

Apostles' Creed

is for us to grow in love. For the principal focus of prayer, which is an act of charity according to St Thomas Aquinas, is to provoke greater devotion for God. And since "nothing can provoke love more than to know that one is loved", so meditating on the Rosary, on what God has lovingly done for man in Christ, is a powerful means of prayer. St Thomas also says that "it is befitting that prayer should last long enough to arouse the fervour of the interior desire: and when it exceeds this measure, so that it cannot be continued any longer without causing weariness, it should be discontinued." The Rosary, it seems to me, is well-suited to this way of praying because we need only pray one decade at a time.

Hence St Louis de Montfort says: "I advise you to divide up your Rosary into three parts and to say each group of mysteries (five decades) at a different time of day. This is much better than saying the whole fifteen decades all at once. If you cannot find the time to say a third part of the Rosary all at one time, say it gradually, a decade here and there. I am sure you can manage this; so that, in spite of your work and all the calls upon your time, you will have said the whole Rosary before going to bed."

Finally, let me just note that "a third part of the Rosary" means five decades, which in Portuguese is called a *Terço*, or in French, a *Chapelet*. The complete fifteen mysteries is called the *Rosário* or *Rosaire*. Unfortunately, we lack this linguistic precision in English. It is interesting, therefore, to note that when Our Lady of the Rosary tells the children at Fatima to say the Rosary every day, Sr Lucia reports that she specifically referred to the *Terço*. Therefore, five decades a day will, for each of us, fulfil our dear Mother's request, her gentle daily prescription to help us keep sin at bay and to increase in holy charity.

CONNECTED IN LOVE THROUGH THE HOLY ROSARY: THE CONFRATERNITY OF THE MOST HOLY ROSARY

Perhaps the most famous saintly promoter of the Holy Rosary is St Louis Marie Grignon de Montfort who was a secular priest and Dominican tertiary who laboured to renew the Faith in 18th century France. In 1712 he obtained permission from the Master of the Dominican Order to preach the Rosary and to enrol members in the Rosary Confraternity. Around this time, St Louis then researched the history and miracles of the Rosary, and he wrote his two books, *True Devotion to the Blessed Virgin* and *The Secret of the Rosary*. Because of the turmoil of the French Revolution and the

resulting anti-Catholicism, both books remained unpublished and were hidden away, literally buried in a field and thus protected by providence from destruction, until they were discovered almost by chance in 1842 and published in 1843.

St Louis de Montfort sums up the great value of the Rosary as Mary's gift to us. He says: "The Holy Rosary teaches people about the virtues of Jesus and Mary and leads them to mental prayer and to imitate Our Lord and Saviour Jesus Christ. It teaches them to approach the sacraments often, genuinely to strive after Christian virtues and to do all kinds of good works, as well as interesting them in the many wonderful indulgences which can be gained through the Rosary." This final point about indulgences highlights the fact that the Rosary, although it is something we can pray alone, is a powerful prayer that unites us with our fellow Christians, drawing upon the merits and graces of the entire communion of saints especially within the Order of Preachers. This is especially true if one is enrolled in the Confraternity of the Holy Rosary, a spiritual association in which Catholics are "banded together in fraternal charity" (Leo XIII).

For it is a beautiful teaching of the Church, often forgotten or neglected in our time, that we Christians are one holy communion of saints such that, as St Paul says: "if one member suffers, all suffer together; if one member is honoured, all rejoice together" (*1 Cor* 12:26). This is one of the effects of our spiritual communion with one another, our union in charity for one another within the Body of Christ that is the Church. Membership in the Confraternity of the Most Holy Rosary especially binds us to one another in love: love for God, love for Our Lady and love for one another. And the common act that we all do which unites us in a spiritual communion is the praying of the Rosary. For the Rosary, devoutly recited, is an act of faith and of love, an act that unites us more perfectly to Christ through Mary.

The only obligation for members of the Rosary Confraternity is to pray fifteen decades of the Rosary each week, meditating on the mysteries of salvation. To become a member, one needs to be enrolled through one of the local Sodalities of the worldwide Confraternity.

For more information, visit: *https://rosaryshrine. co.uk/rosary-shrine/rosary-confraternity/*
Or email: *rosarium@curia.op.org*

Further Marian Prayers

Tradition holds that the Holy Rosary was a gift from Our Lady to St Dominic and thus to the whole Church, and we know that it is the recommended prayer of Our Lady of the Rosary at Fatima to her beloved children. However, over the centuries, and particularly in the Middle Ages as Marian devotion flowered in the Western Church, there have arisen a host of prayers offered by the Church and her saints to Our Lady. The Rosary itself and its name which suggests a garland of flowers offered to one's beloved is also something we offer to Our Blessed Mother with love, devotion and fidelity. In addition to the Rosary, I offer here a selection of the most beautiful prayers to Our Lady from the Church's treasury, some of which are particular to our Dominican tradition and so differ slightly from the version you might already know.

The Angelus

The *Angelus*, which recalls the cosmos-changing moment of the Lord's Incarnation in Our Lady's womb, is much loved by the Dominicans. For by his becoming Man, God affirms the goodness of all creation and matter, and meditating on the pregnancy of Mary was a counterfoil to the anti-family, anti-life Albigensian heresy which St Dominic encountered and preached against in the 13th century. The famous Dominican convent of San Marco in Florence thus has a beautiful fresco of the Annunciation painted at the top of the stairs leading to the cells (bedrooms) of the friars, with an inscription telling them to pray the Angelus and so to ponder the Incarnation before they went to bed.

The current custom in the Church is to pray the *Angelus* at dawn (usually at 6am), at noon and in the evening (usually at 6pm).

* * *

V. Angelus Domini nuntiavit Mariæ.
R. Et concepit de Spiritu Sancto.
V. Ave Maria …   R. Sancta Maria …
V. Ecce ancilla Domini.
R. Fiat mihi secundum verbum tuum.
V. Ave Maria …   R. Sancta Maria …
V. (genuflect) Et Verbum caro factum est.
R. Et habitavit in nobis.
V. Ave Maria …   R. Sancta Maria …
V. Ora pro nobis, sancta Dei Genetrix.
R. Ut digni efficiamur promissionibus Christi.

Oremus.
Gratiam tuam, quæsumus Domine, mentibus nostris infunde; ut qui, angelo nuntiante, Christi Filii tui incarnationem cognovimus, per passionem eius et crucem ad resurrectionis gloriam perducamur. Per eundem Christum Dominum nostrum.
R. Amen.

V. The Angel of the Lord declared unto Mary.
R. And she conceived by the Holy Spirit.
V. Hail Mary …   R. Holy Mary …
V. Behold the handmaid of the Lord.
R. Be it done unto me according to thy word.
V. Hail Mary …   R. Holy Mary …
V. (genuflect) And the Word became flesh.
R. And dwelt amongst us.
V. Hail Mary …   R. Holy Mary …
V. Pray for us, O holy Mother of God.
R. That we may be made worthy of the promises of Christ.

Let us pray.
Pour forth, we beseech thee O Lord, thy grace into our hearts, that we to whom the Incarnation of Christ thy Son was made known by the message of an angel, may by his Passion and Cross be brought to the glory of his Resurrection. Through the same Christ our Lord.
R. Amen.

Salve Regina

The *Salve Regina*, or Hail Holy Queen, is the valedictory salutation to Our Lady, usually said at the close of the Rosary. Since the time of St Bernard this anthem had been sung at the end of Compline, at the close of the day. However in 1221, Blessed Jordan of Saxony, the second Master of the Dominican Order, asked the friars in Bologna to process to the altar of Our Lady while singing the *Salve Regina* after Compline. The *Salve* procession is an important and beautiful part of our Dominican heritage, and several people reported seeing Our Lady appear at this time to bless the friars with holy water and to intercede with Christ for the protection of her Order, the Friars Preachers. This anthem is the first that we learn as Dominican novices and the last that we hear, because as a friar lies in his death bed, his brothers will come and gather around to sing it, like a lullaby to sing the dying friar to eternal rest in Our Lady's arms.

* * *

Salve, Regina, mater misericordiæ; vita, dulcedo, et spes nostra, salve. Ad te clamamus, exsules filii Evæ. Ad te suspiramus, gementes et flentes in hac lacrimarum valle. Eia ergo, advocata nostra, illos tuos misericordes oculos ad nos converte. Et Iesum, benedictum fructum ventris tui, nobis post hoc exsilium ostende. O clemens, O pia, O dulcis Virgo Maria.

V. Dignare me laudare te, Virgo sacrata.
R. Da mihi virtutem contra hostes tuos.

Oremus.
Concede nos famulos tuos, quæsumus, Domine Deus, perpetua mentis et corporis salute gaudere: et gloriosa beatæ Mariæ semper Virginis intercessione, a presenti liberari tristitia et æterna perfrui lætitia. Per Christum Dominum nostrum. R. Amen.

Hail, holy Queen, mother of mercy, hail, our life, our sweetness and our hope. To thee do we cry, poor banished children of Eve. To thee do we send up our sighs, mourning and weeping in this vale of tears. Turn then, O most gracious advocate, thine eyes of mercy toward us and after this exile show unto us the blessed fruit of thy womb, Jesus. O clement, O loving, O sweet Virgin Mary.

V. Give me grace to praise thee, Holy Virgin
R. Give me strength against thine enemies.

Let us pray.
Grant to us, thy servants, Lord, unfailing health of mind and body; and through the prayers of the Blessed Virgin Mary in her glory, free us from our sorrows in this life and grant us eternal happiness in the next. Through Christ our Lord.
R. Amen.

Regina Cæli

According to *The Golden Legend*, a great

medieval bestseller of the lives of the Saints compiled by the Dominican bishop Bl. James of Varagine (Jacobus de Voragine), this anthem in honour of Our Lady, sung during Eastertide, was first heard being proclaimed by angelic voices when Pope St Gregory the Great was leading a procession in Rome in the 6th century, seeking relief from pestilence for the city. As this penitential procession made its way through the city, they carried at the front an icon of Our Lady said to have been painted by St Luke. This icon was, presumably, the one now called the "Madonna of San Sisto", a most sublime image of Our Lady that St Dominic had carried from the monastery of San Sisto, and which is now in the care of the Dominican nuns in Monte Mario, near the Vatican.

* * *

V. Regina cæli, lætare. Alleluia.
R. Quia quem meruisti portare. Alleluia.
V. Resurrexit, sicut dixit. Alleluia.
R. Ora pro nobis Deum. Alleluia.
V. Gaude et lætare, Virgo Maria. Alleluia.
R. Quia surrexit Dominus vere. Alleluia.

Oremus.
Deus, qui per resurrectionem Filii tui, Domini nostri Iesu Christi, mundum lætificare dignatus es: præsta, quæsumus, ut per eius Genitricem Virginem Mariam, perpetuæ capiamus gaudia vitæ. Per eundem Christum Dominum nostrum.
R. Amen.
V. Queen of heaven, rejoice! Alleluia.
R. For he whom you did merit to bear. Alleluia.
V. Has risen, as he said. Alleluia.

R. Pray to God for us. Alleluia.
V. Rejoice and be glad, O Virgin Mary. Alleluia.
R. For the Lord is truly risen. Alleluia.

Let us pray.
O God, you have been pleased to gladden the world by the Resurrection of your Son, our Lord Jesus Christ; grant, we pray, that through his mother, the Virgin Mary, we may receive the joys of everlasting life. Through the same Christ our Lord.
R. Amen.

Litany of the Blessed Virgin Mary
Received by the Order of Preachers

Many of the earliest stories about the Order of

Ave Regina Cælorum
(Dominican Use)

Although this Marian anthem is commonly used during Lent, there was an old Dominican tradition of singing this anthem after Compline in place of the *Salve Regina*, probably as it was written sometime in the 12th century and grew in popularity in the early years of the Order. A variant of this prayer arose in the Order which is very slightly different from the received text used universally, but we Dominicans still say our own version of this beautiful anthem.

* * *

Ave Regina Cælorum
Ave Domina Angelorum
Salve, radix sancta ex qua mundo lux est orta:
Gaude, gloriosa, super omnes speciosa,
Vale, valde decora,
Et pro nobis semper Christum exora.

Hail, Queen of Heaven
Hail, Lady of Angels
Hail holy root from whom the Light of the World has arisen:
Rejoice, O glorious one,
Lovely beyond all others.
Farewell, most beautiful one,
And ever pray for us to Christ.

Sub tuum præsidium

Recent research has traced this succinct prayer to a Greek text dating to the 3rd century, making it the oldest extant prayer to Our Lady. In the Dominican Liturgy, it is used as the *Nunc dimittis* antiphon at Compline on certain feasts of Our Lady, and it is also sung while kneeling on Saturdays.

* * *

Sub tuum præsidium confugimus, sancta Dei Genetrix; nostras deprecationes ne despicias in necessitatibus nostris, sed a periculis cunctis libera nos semper, Virgo gloriosa et benedicta.

We fly to your patronage, O holy Mother of God. Despise not our petitions in our necessities, but deliver us from all dangers, O ever-glorious and blessed Virgin.

Alma Redemptoris Mater

One of the earliest manuscripts of this anthem to Our Lady, which is customarily taken up from Advent and throughout the Christmas season, is found in the monastery of Dominican nuns in Basel that dates to sometime between 1437–1442. Full of wonder at the Incarnation and Birth of the Saviour, this anthem gives us pause at the close of the day to ponder the mysteries of Christmastide, the joyful mysteries of our salvation. The translation given here was made by St John Henry Newman.

* * *

Alma Redemptoris Mater quæ pervia cæli porta manes, et stella maris, succurre cadenti, surgere qui curat, populo: tu quæ genuisti, natura mirante, tuum sanctum Genitorem, Virgo prius ac posterius, Gabrielis ab ore sumens illud Ave, peccatorum miserere.

Kindly Mother of the Redeemer, who art ever of heaven, the open gate and the star of the sea, aid a fallen people, which is trying to rise again; thou who didst give birth, while nature marvelled how, to thy Holy Creator, Virgin both before and after, from Gabriel's mouth accepting the All hail, be merciful towards sinners.

Preachers affirm that the Dominicans were a special fruit of Mary's prayers; that they enjoyed her protection and wore the white scapular she gave them; and that she blessed them every night when they sang the *Salve Regina*. In the 1250s, the nascent Order was under threat as secular clergy and university professors both strove to halt the popularity and success of the Order of Preachers by severely restricting the rights of the friars to preach and beg for alms. In response, Blessed Humbert of Romans, the fifth Master of the Order, turned to Our Lady and begged for her help and protection. This Litany of Our Lady has come down to us in the Dominican tradition and is believed to date from this trying period in the Order's history. So, in times of difficulty and persecution and trial, the Dominican Order still has recourse to the Blessed Virgin Mary and takes up in prayer this medieval Litany which has several very beautiful and striking invocations. So powerful and efficacious is this Litany that some have remarked: "Be careful with the Litanies of the Friars Preachers—they work wonders"!

* * *

V. Deus in adiutorium meum intende.
R. Domine ad adiuvandum me festina.

V. Kyrie, eleison.
R. Kyrie, eleison.
V. Christe, eleison.
R. Christe, eleison.
V. Kyrie, eleison.
R. Kyrie, eleison.
V. Christe, audi nos.
R. Christe, audi nos.
V. Christe, exaudi nos.
R. Christe, exaudi nos.

V. Pater de cælis Deus,
R. miserere nobis.
V. Fili Redemptor mundi Deus,
R. miserere nobis.
V. Spiritus Sancte Deus,
R. miserere nobis.
V. Sancta Trinitas, unus Deus,
R. miserere nobis.

V. O God, come to my assistance.
R. Lord, make haste to help me.

V. Lord, have mercy.
R. Lord, have mercy.
V. Christ, have mercy.
R. Christ, have mercy.
V. Lord, have mercy.
R. Lord have mercy.
V. Christ, hear us.
R. Christ, hear us.
V. Christ, graciously hear us.
R. Christ, graciously hear us.

V. God the Father in Heaven,
R. have mercy on us.
V. God the Son, Redeemer of the world,
R. have mercy on us.
V. God the Holy Spirit,
R. have mercy on us.

Sancta Maria,   R. ora pro nobis.
Sancta Maria Mater Christi sanctissima,
Sancta Maria Dei Genitrix Virgo,
Sancta Maria Mater innupta,
Sancta Maria Mater inviolata,
Sancta Maria Virgo virginum,
Sancta Maria Virgo perpetua,
Sancta Maria gratia Dei plena,
Sancta Maria æterni Regis filia,
Sancta Maria Christi Mater et Sponsa,
Sancta Maria Spiritus Sancti Templum,
Sancta Maria Cælorum Regina,
Sancta Maria Angelorum Domina,
Sancta Maria scala Dei,
Sancta Maria porta Paradisi,
Sancta Maria nostra Mater et Domina,
Sancta Maria nostra spes vera,
Sancta Maria nova Mater,
Sancta Maria omnium fidelium fides,
Sancta Maria caritas Dei perfecta,
Sancta Maria imperatrix nostra,
Sancta Maria fons dulcedinis,
Sancta Maria Mater Misericordiæ,
Sancta Maria Mater æterni Principis,
Sancta Maria Mater veri consilii,
Sancta Maria Mater veræ fidei,
Sancta Maria nostra resurrectio,
Sancta Maria per quam renovatur omnis creatura,
Sancta Maria generans æternum Lumen,
Sancta Maria omnia portantem portans,
Sancta Maria virtus divinæ Incarnationis,
Sancta Maria cubile thesauri cælestis,
Sancta Maria generans factorem omnium,
Sancta Maria consilii cælestis arcanum,

V. Holy Trinity, one God,
R. have mercy on us.

Holy Mary,   R. pray for us.
Holy Mary, most holy Mother of Christ,
Holy Mary, Virgin Mother of God,
Holy Mary, maiden Mother,
Holy Mary, Mother inviolate,
Holy Mary, Virgin of virgins,
Holy Mary, ever Virgin,
Holy Mary, full of the grace of God,
Holy Mary, daughter of the eternal King,
Holy Mary, Mother and Bride of Christ,
Holy Mary, Temple of the Holy Spirit,
Holy Mary, Queen of Heaven,
Holy Mary, Lady of the Angels,
Holy Mary, ladder of God,
Holy Mary, door of Heaven,
Holy Mary, our Mother and Lady,
Holy Mary, our true hope,
Holy Mary, new Mother,
Holy Mary, faith of all the faithful,
Holy Mary, perfect charity of God,
Holy Mary, our empress,
Holy Mary, font of sweetness,
Holy Mary, Mother of Mercy,
Holy Mary, Mother of the everlasting Prince,
Holy Mary, Mother of good counsel,
Holy Mary, Mother of true faith,
Holy Mary, our resurrection,
Holy Mary, through whom all creatures are renewed,
Holy Mary, who brings forth the eternal Light,
Holy Mary, bearer of the Bearer of all,
Holy Mary, strength of the divine Incarnation,
Holy Mary, chamber of heavenly treasures,

Sancta Maria nostra salus vera,	Holy Mary, who brings forth the Maker of all,
Sancta Maria thesaurus fidelium,	Holy Mary, secret of heavenly counsel,
Sancta Maria pulcherrima Domina,	Holy Mary, our true salvation,
Sancta Maria iris plena lætitia,	Holy Mary, treasure of the faithful,
Sancta Maria Mater veri gaudii,	Holy Mary, Lady most fair,
Sancta Maria iter nostrum ad Dominum,	Holy Mary, rainbow full of joy,
Sancta Maria advocatrix nostra,	Holy Mary, Mother of true rejoicing,
Sancta Maria stella cæli clarissima,	Holy Mary, our path to the Lord,
Sancta Maria præclarior luna,	Holy Mary, our advocate,
Sancta Maria solem lumine vincens,	Holy Mary, star most bright of the heavens,
Sancta Maria æterni Dei Mater,	Holy Mary, more illustrious than the moon,
Sancta Maria delens tenebras æternae noctis,	Holy Mary, overwhelming the sun with light,
Sancta Maria delens chyrographum nostræ perditionis,	Holy Mary, Mother of Eternal God,
Sancta Maria fons veræ sapientiæ,	Holy Mary, destroying the darkness of eternal night,
Sancta Maria lumen rectæ scientiæ,	Holy Mary, blotting out the decree of our damnation,
Sancta Maria inæstimabile gaudium nostrum,	Holy Mary, font of true wisdom,
Sancta Maria præmium nostrum,	Holy Mary, light of right knowledge,
Sancta Maria cælestis patriæ desiderium,	Holy Mary, our inestimable joy,
Sancta Maria speculum divinæ contemplationis,	Holy Mary, our prize,
Sancta Maria omnium Beatorum beatissima,	Holy Mary, desire of the heavenly homeland,
Sancta Maria omni laude dignissima,	Holy Mary, mirror of divine contemplation,
Sancta Maria clementissima Domina,	Holy Mary, most blessed of all the Blessed,
Sancta Maria consolatrix ad te confugientium,	Holy Mary, most worthy of all praise,
Sancta Maria plena pietate,	Holy Mary, most clement Lady,
Sancta Maria omni dulcedine superabundans,	Holy Mary, consoler of all who fly to thee,
Sancta Maria pulchritudo angelorum,	Holy Mary, full of pity,
Sancta Maria flos patriarcharum,	Holy Mary, overflowing with all sweetness,
Sancta Maria humilitas prophetarum,	Holy Mary, beauty of the angels,
Sancta Maria thesaurus apostolorum,	Holy Mary, flower of the patriarchs,
Sancta Maria laus martyrum,	Holy Mary, humility of the prophets,
Sancta Maria glorificatio sacerdotum,	Holy Mary, treasure of the apostles,
Sancta Maria decus virginum,	Holy Mary, praise of martyrs,
Sancta Maria castitatis lilium,	Holy Mary, glorification of priests,
Sancta Maria super omnes feminas benedicta,	Holy Mary, beauty of virgins,
Sancta Maria reparatio omnium perditorum,	Holy Mary, lily of chastity,

Sancta Maria laus omnium iustorum,
Sancta Maria secretorum Dei conscia,
Sancta Maria sanctissima omnium feminarum,
Sancta Maria præclarissima Domina,
Sancta Maria margarita cælestis Sponsi,
Sancta Maria palatium Christi,
Sancta Maria Immaculata Virgo,
Sancta Maria templum Domini,
Sancta Maria gloria Ierusalem,
Sancta Maria lætitia Israel,
Sancta Maria filia Dei,
Sancta Maria sponsa Christi amantissima,
Sancta Maria stella maris,
Sancta Maria diadema in capite summi Regis,
Sancta Maria omni honore dignissima,
Sancta Maria omni dulcedine plena,
Sancta Maria regni cælestis meritum,
Sancta Maria cælestis vitae ianua,
Sancta Maria porta clausa et patens,
Sancta Maria per quam intratur ad Dominum,
Sancta Maria immarcescibilis rosa,
Sancta Maria omni mundo pretiosior,
Sancta Maria omni thesauro desiderabilior,
Sancta Maria altior cælo,
Sancta Maria angelis mundior,
Sancta Maria archangelorum lætitia,
Sancta Maria omnium sanctorum exsultatio,
Sancta Maria honor, et laus, et gloria, et fiducia nostra,
Sancta Maria extende manum tuam et tange cor
    nostrum, ut illumines et liberes nos peccatores,

V. Filia Dei, Maria,
R. nos respice.
V. Filia Ioachim, Maria,
R. nos dilige.

Holy Mary, blessed above all women,
Holy Mary, recourse of those who are lost,
Holy Mary, praise of all the just,
Holy Mary, knower of the secrets of God,
Holy Mary, most holy of all women,
Holy Mary, most noble Lady,
Holy Mary, pearl of the heavenly Spouse,
Holy Mary, palace of Christ,
Holy Mary, Immaculate Virgin,
Holy Mary, temple of the Lord,
Holy Mary, glory of Jerusalem,
Holy Mary, joy of Israel,
Holy Mary, daughter of God,
Holy Mary, most beloved spouse of Christ,
Holy Mary, star of the sea,
Holy Mary, diadem on the head of the sovereign King,
Holy Mary, most worthy of all honour,
Holy Mary, full of all sweetness,
Holy Mary, reward of the heavenly kingdom,
Holy Mary, gate of heavenly life,
Holy Mary, door both closed and open,
Holy Mary, through whom we come to the Lord,
Holy Mary, rose that cannot wilt,
Holy Mary, more precious than the whole world,
Holy Mary, more desirable than all treasure,
Holy Mary, higher than heaven,
Holy Mary, purer than the angels,
Holy Mary, joy of the archangels,
Holy Mary, exaltation of all saints,
Holy Mary, our honour, praise, glory and trust,
Holy Mary, extend your hand and touch our hearts,
    that you may enlighten us sinners,

V. Holy Mary, daughter of God,
R. look upon us.
V. Holy Mary, daughter of Joachim,

V. Filia Annæ, Maria,
R. nos suscipe.
V. Agna Dei, tu porta spei,
R. porta nos ad Filium.
V. Agna Dei, nos iungas ei,
R. virginale lilium.
V. Agna Dei, da requiei regnum,
R. post exilium.

V. Ora pro nobis, Sancta Dei Genetrix.
R. Ut digni efficiamur promissionibus Christi.

V. Dignare me laudare te, Virgo sacrata.
R. Da mihi virtutem contra hostes tuos.

V. Domine, exaudi orationem meam.
R. Et clamor meus ad te veniat.

Oratio
Defende, quæsumus, Domine Deus, intercedente beata et gloriosa Dei Genetrice Maria cum omnibus sanctis tuis, nostram ab omni adversitate Domum et Ordinem, et ab hostium tuere clementer insidiis.
Per Christum Dominum nostrum.
R. Amen.

R. love us.
V. Holy Mary, daughter of Anne,
R. receive us.
V. She-lamb of God, gateway of hope,
R. carry us to your Son,
V. She-lamb of God, join us to him,
R. virginal lily.
V. She-lamb of God, give us the rest of the Kingdom,
R. after this our exile.

V. Pray for us, O Holy Mother of God,
R. That we may be made worthy of the promises of Christ.

V. Make me worthy to praise you, Sacred Virgin.
R. Strengthen me against your enemies.

V. O Lord, hear my prayer.
R. And let my cry come unto you.

Prayer
We beseech you, Lord God, that through the intercession of the blessed and glorious ever-Virgin Mary and all your saints, that you defend from all adversity our house and our Order and that you protect it from all the snares of our enemies.
Through Christ our Lord.
R. Amen.

* * *

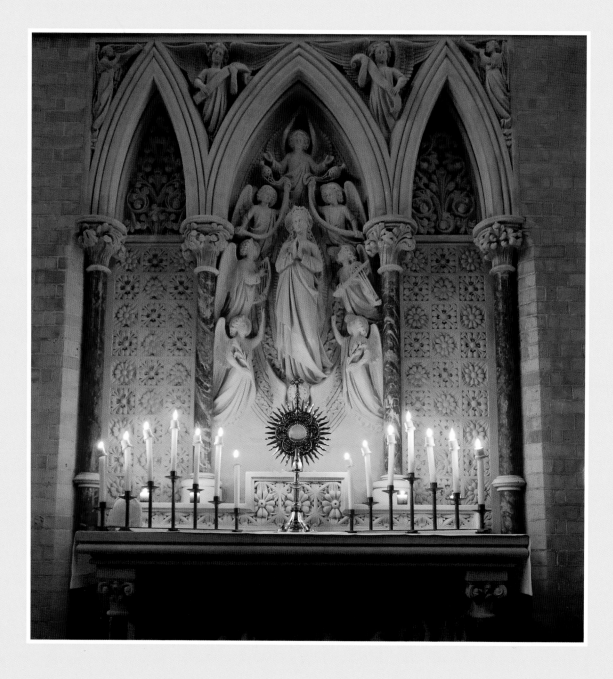

IMAGE CAPTIONS

Page 2: *The Madonna of San Sisto* which is in the custody of the Dominican nuns in Monte Mario, Rome. This miraculous icon is believed to be the earliest painted image of Our Lady.

Page 7: 5th century mosaic of the Annunciation from the Basilica of St Mary Major in Rome.

Page 9: Mosaic of Pope St Pius V from the Rosary Altar in the 19th century Rosary Shrine church (St Dominic's Priory) in London.

Page 12: Stained glass window from the church of St Pius V in Providence, RI (USA).

Page 13: The Rosary Garden of the Rosary Shrine church (St Dominic's Priory) in London.

Page 62: Dominican friars lead a Marian procession in Walsingham, the national Marian Shrine of England.

Page 64: Stained glass window in the Dominican nuns chapel at Buffalo, NY (USA).

Page 65: The Dominican family taking part in the Rosary Procession in Lourdes.

Page 66: Tympanum over the entrance to the Rosary Basilica, Lourdes.

Page 67: Stained glass window in the Dominican church in Dubrovnik, Croatia.

Page 72: Fresco in the cell of St Dominic in the priory of Santa Sabina, Rome.

Page 78: The Assumption chapel in the 19th century Rosary Shrine church (St Dominic's Priory) in London.

All images © Lawrence Lew, O.P.

The Joyful Mysteries

Carved stone reredos in the Annunciation Chapel of the 19th century Rosary Shrine church (St Dominic's Priory) in London, U.K.

The Visitation by Luca della Robbia, made in Florence ca.1445. It is in the church of San Leone in Pistoia, Italy.

Nativity Window, installed in 1910. It was designed by Edward Burne-Jones and executed by William Morris in Winchester Cathedral, U.K.

Detail from the oak reredos in the chapel of the Dominican House of Studies in Washington D.C., U.S.A. Carved in Ghent (Belgium), the main altar with its reredos of the Rosary mysteries was in place by 1907.

Stained glass window from the Chapel of the Mercy Sisters Convent of St Catharine in Edinburgh, U.K.

The Sorrowful Mysteries

Votive chapel in the National Shrine of St Elizabeth Ann Seton in Emmitsburg, Maryland, U.S.A.

Statue in the chapel of Mount Aloysius College in Cresson, Pennsylvania, U.S.A.

Carved stone reredos in the Crowning with Thorns Chapel of the 19th century Rosary Shrine church (St Dominic's Priory) in London, U.K.

One of the Stations of the Cross from the Sanctuary of Lourdes in France.

Fresco of *The Crucifixion and St Dominic* painted c.1441–42 by Bl John of Fiesole O.P. (Fra Angelico), in the cloister of San Marco in Florence.

The Glorious Mysteries

6th century mosaic from the church of Sant'Apollinare Nuovo in Ravenna, Italy.

19th century stained glass window from the Cathedral of the Blessed Sacrament in Altoona, Pennsylvania, U.S.A.

Carved stone reredos in the Pentecost Chapel of the 19th century Rosary Shrine church (St Dominic's Priory) in London, U.K.

Carved stone retable of the 18th century High Altar by Charles-Antoine Bridan in Chartres Cathedral, France.

Stained glass window in the Cathedral Basilica of the Assumption, Covington, Kentucky, U.S.A.

THE LUMINOUS MYSTERIES

Main altarpiece in the Co-Cathedral of St John the Baptist in Valletta, Malta. It was sculpted by Giuseppe Mazzuoli in 1703.

Our Lady of Cana sculpted by Cody Swanson in 2018 for the Mysteries of Light Rosary Garden at the Rosary Shrine (St Dominic's Priory) in London, U.K.

Early 20th century stained glass window designed by Frederick Stymetz Lamb and installed in the Stanford Memorial Church in Stanford, California, U.S.A.

Apse mosaic in the 20th century Church of the Transfiguration by Antonio Baluzzi. It is built on the summit of Mount Tabor in Israel, the traditional site of the Lord's Transfiguration.

Stained glass window in the Cathedral Basilica of Saint-Brieuc in Brittany, France.